A World Within The Wind

Roni Ann Wilkerson

A World Within The Wind © 2023 Roni Ann Wilkerson

All rights reserved.

No part of this publication may be reproduced, stored in a retrieval system, or transmitted, in any form or by any means, electronic, mechanical, photocopying, recording or otherwise, without the prior written permission of the presenters.

Roni Ann Wilkerson asserts the moral right to be identified as author of this work.

Presentation by *BookLeaf Publishing*

Web: www.bookleafpub.com

E-mail: info@bookleafpub.com

ISBN: 9789358368185

First edition 2023

To my Davy, always create beautiful memories. Remember that without pain, we wouldn't understand happiness. Mama loves you infinitely and I am proud of you just for existing. Mama loves you beyond words.

ACKNOWLEDGEMENT

Book Leaf Publishing has given me a wonderful opportunity and made this book possible. I will eternally be grateful and hope to work with them again in the future.

Terry and Carol Myres: my father and mother always believed in me. They taught me to read very early and encouraged my writing. They have been the world class example of how to encourage your children to follow their heart's ambition. I strive to be like them for my child. "Thank you" is not enough to suffice.

David: How do I begin to find the words to thank the man who has literally given me the world? I told you my 3 biggest dreams in life and you've made them happen. You took me to the ocean for the first time. You and I became parents to our masterpiece, Davy. And you not only encouraged but help fund my traveling and quite literally "gave me the world". Your help with this book has been tremendous and you missed hours of sleep listening to me fret but also my excitement. Words are not enough.

My Davy: You are the light of my life. Your laughter is my favorite song. Seeing the world in your eyes is opening mine to the richness of nature all around us. Thank you for choosing me in the premortal existence to be your mother. I would always choose you, too. I love you infinitely.

Eray Dinç: You have helped make me a better person. Without you, I would have never learned about Türkiye and I would not have had the opportunity to make such beautiful memories. Thank you for the soul connection, the memories that are etched permanently and for believing in me. You helped me see my own beauty and recognize my own worth. I'm eternally grateful for all the inspiration.

Ali Sait Malkoç: You have been my friend through some of life's hardest lessons. We are friends for life and you supported and encouraged me to write this book from the start. You believe I have talent and you helped motivate me. When I needed inspiration, you gave me the idea behind my poem, "Allah's Love". Your idea inspired me to go on and write many new poems. Thank you for being my biggest motivator.

Richard Appelbaum: You've always believed in me and we have been friends since our first semester in college. You've let me bounce ideas off of you and you've given me the right amounts of criticism and encouragement. Thank you for always giving your honest views.

Kurtuluş Lütfi Yavuz: You haven't been my friend as long as many but you've always supported and encouraged me. No matter the topic, you've been positive and you stood by me during some of my heartaches. You immediately believed I could write this and shared your thoughts and ideas. You might already be my biggest fan. Thank you, my friend.

To all of my friends who believe in me and encourage me... I would be lost without you all.

To my ancestors: I hope I make you proud and you see elements of yourself in my work.

To the great poets who inspired me and the new ambitious ones that I continue to find... Poetry is an art. Thank you for sharing and baring your soul to us all.

PREFACE

"There is no place in the world where you can see views like this," the wise older man on the ferry on the Bosphorus said next to me. He spoke of his life in business and of all the places he traveled. He asked why I was in Türkiye and he encouraged me to write my memories to enjoy in my golden years. We discussed life and love and the man seemed to disappear once we exited the ferry but his words lingered. He told my friend the same words I had said many times... "You can't find a place like this in America." He's right.

The first time I sat by the Aegean sea and we watched the sunset, I said to my friend "the mountains seem to kiss the sea." Watching the sunrise over the Sea of Marmara and sitting by the lighthouse, I once again felt the stir to want to write the memories. Days later, we met a beautiful woman on the beaches of Erdek and she was a poet selling her books. As we read our books and sipped coffee, I reflected in this. I would love to be that woman some day.

Türkiye changed me. I felt like my soul was now a duality. There was "American Roni", the woman I've always been. The woman proud of her Native American heritage and who studied ancestry, had climbed the ranks to the top of her career, and who had always been devouted to family and now a mother. But there was also "Turkish Roni," who rekindled old passions of writing, learning language and culture, focused on religion and found new sense of self worth. How do you combine these? The answer is simple. Writing allows me to coexist in both worlds and merge to become a new and more whole soul.

If you listen to the wind, you can hear whispers from the ancestors but dreams of the future. You can create your own world within the wind.

Coffee

As the rain is falling
The fresh smell teleports me away...
Now I'm on a balcony,
The cool rain splashing onto my face
As I watch the children playing in the street...
You quietly come behind me.
I can feel your breath on my neck,
Your warm chest nestling against my back,
Your heart beating in your chest,
Your strong arms wrapping around my hips,
Your voice is like music
"Coffee", you say
You are quickly gone again and I am
memorizing this moment
Smells envelope and engulf me
The aroma of fresh rain,
The scent of bread that is baked two blocks
away,
The world smells new and clean.
You reappear with coffee for both of us.
As I sip and watch the rain,
You wrap a blanket around us both.
"Imagine if it were snow" you say
We continue to watch the rain
Lost in the moment

But then I blink
I'm back home.
That memory was strong and lingers
I feel a chill down my back and a painful reminder
I continue to watch the falling rain
But it falls like lonely tears
There is no balcony
No sound of children's laughter or splashing
Just the drops silently falling
You are not here
Your warmth...
Your voice...
But then I hear the wind whisper
"Coffee"

Life's Ashes

Ashes are everywhere
The air is so heavy
Why am I here?
Is this real?
Days before I had started packing
My house is boxes
But now I stand in my charred kitchen
Everything is gone
I have lost it all
How did I get here?
The air is so heavy
Should I have died?
Am I dead?
No.
I am sick
I've been sick
My puppy died and I got sick
I stayed at my Mother's house
The air is so heavy
Am I dead?
Memories flash but I feel the kitchen counter behind me
It's cool to the touch and I feel grounded
The air is so heavy
Open the door

But the walls barely stand
Ashes
My life entirely gone
Think.
Am I dead?
No.
Your husband didn't want you
You've been sick
Your best friend moved away
Your puppy died
You are all alone
Your Father faught with you
You should have been here
Was I here?
Am I dead?
I feel nothing.
The air is so heavy
Ashes everywhere
Think.
They say your house exploded
You would have surely died
But your Mother asked you to stay the night
Why did I listen?
Now everything is gone
I should be gone
Yesterday I showed my cherished memories
A pink and white monkey sweater
My first stuffed animals
A shirt that belonged to Grandmother

Now all gone
Pictures
Family heirlooms
Gone.
The air is so heavy
Everything is gone
And ashes are all that remain
I stand here in silence
Deafening silence
Everything is gone.
My husband - gone.
Best friend - gone.
Earthly possessions - gone.
My car doesn't run - gone.
I've been sick and lost my job - gone.
My puppy - gone.
House plants - gone.
Why am I here?
The doctor says I have three months to live
But what is this?
Is this living?
Ashes
Three months to live in ashes?
I have no one
I have nothing
I will die and leave nothing
The air is so heavy
"God? Are you there?"
My voice shakes

The deafening silence
The air is so heavy
Sweat enters my forehead
I walk through the house
Climb over roof pieces
See the place where I should have died
"God, why am I here?"
Silence and ashes
Do I deserve to suffer?
My last days alone
With nothing
It's already a painful death
But the explosion was quick
The smoke would have taken me in seconds
But why wasn't I here?
The air is so heavy
My name
Am I hallucinating?
Did I just hear my name?
I need air,
I should go
But should I die here?
I could lay down
I could die here.
Who would find me?
My name again
The air is so heavy
No one is here.
Maybe the smoke makes me crazy

There is a light
It's brighter
I'm not scared.
Is this death?
The air is heavy
Am I alone?
"I've always been with you."
"Who said that?", I ask
Ashes and silence
"God didn't bring you this far to leave you now."
It's direct.
It's firm.
It's clear.
"Are you Jesus?"
The light is now gone
Ashes and silence
The air is heavy
I need to get out
I walk out the door but turn to look
My life is all ashes
Ashes and silence
But I am not alone...

Cosmic Dance

Our souls intertwined in cosmic dance,
A meeting of spirits in perfect chance,
Together we spark, ignite, and glow,
A love so true, passions overflow.

But you chose deception and deceit.
A betrayal so cold, left me incomplete,
The wind so deep, scars will never heal,
Broken trust, hearts lost to feel.

Everytime I try to say farewell
The universe beckons, as if to tell,
Our souls forever fused by fate,
A bond so strong, can never abate.

The stars align with every step,
Our souls connected, we can't forget,
Though miles apart, we remain as one,
Invisible bonds, that can't be undone.

The passing of time, can never break,
The bond we share, it will never shake,
So we dance again, in the cosmic scheme,
A love so deep, like a waking dream.

Thoughts in the Wind

Under crescent moon, gazing at the sea,
Our hearts beat in tune, wild and free,
But now there's an ocean, vast and blue,
Separating our love, me and you.

- the wind blows -

Our souls, our artwork divine,
A masterpiece of endless design.
Our hearts, woven as one,
A tapestry by love undone.

- the wind blows -

The poet of time, he breathes
Words that dance like autumn leaves
Love and politics, they collide
In his verses, they coincide

Nature whispers in his ear
Guides his pen without fear
Forever entranced by his rhyme
The poet of time, awakens time.

- the wind blows -

Lost in the tangle of life's web
My soulmate, now a distant neb
A flower plucked before it can bloom
Left to dwell in a silent tomb

Our union was a symphony
Now just a faint memory
Like two notes that once entwined
Now separated, undefined.

- the wind blows -

Soulmate betrayed me, tore my heart apart,
Yet life keeps bringing us together,
We dance around each other in the dark,
Bound by fate, our love a tether.

I thought we were meant to be,
Destined to walk through life hand in hand,
Now it's just painful irony,
As we remain intertwined like sand.

The betrayal cuts deep like a knife,
But time has a way of healing wounds,
Our tumultuous journey like a strife,
Where love is lost and then found anew soon.

Despite it all, my heart still beats,

For the one who caused me so much pain,
My love for you will never deplete,
As we meet again and again.

Seasons change, as do we,
And yet we always find our way back,
Our love like a turbulent sea,
Endlessly moving, yet never off track.

You are like the sun on a summer morn,
Beautiful, warm, and full of light,
Even as we're battered and torn,
Our souls remain connected tight.

Life is a cycle of ups and downs,
A never-ending dance of death and birth,
But through it all, we remain bound,
Our love a constant on this earth.

The Mulberry Tree

The tea still burns the tongue,
And we melt under the mulberry tree.
Sipping until our throats are wrung,
None can outlast memories in our plea.

Underneath the branches of fate,
We sit and ponder what's to come,
Glimpses of the future we await,
But in the end, we succumb.

The sun sets behind the hills,
And we watch the sky turn crimson,
A world of beauty that always thrills,
But in it's grandeur, we are imprisoned.

The tea still burns the tongue,
And we melt under the mulberry tree.
Every moment passed seems so young,
Yet, we cannot halt destiny.

As the stars come into sight,
We realize how we've grown,
The days and years take flight,
And we can't help but feel alone.

The tea stills burns the tongue,
And we melt under the mulberry tree,
We yearn for our youth, newly spurned,
But time's inevitable, it has to be.

The cycle of life and death,
Symbolized by nature's constant flow,
We know not what's to come next,
But life must continue on, we know.

The tea still burns the tongue,
And we melt under the mulberry tree,
The memories stay in our lungs,
As we live life fully and free.

Davy's Mother

Every day I prayed and begged
For this one ambition- to be a mother
To hold you close and keep you safe
To feel your tiny heartbeat under my palm.

The sound of your laughter became my song
The feel of your cheek against my own
Became my favourite sensation
And every moment we shared was a gift.

I remember how you climbed up on my ribs
And settled there, content
And how you didn't want to leave
The sound of my heart and my voice.

Even during those long nights
When sleep was just a fading dream
And my arms were tired from holding you close
I felt blessed to have you there with me.

Your first cry was fragile and small
And my heart ached with love and worry.
But then the doctor said, "Here's your baby,"
And you opened your eyes and I was the first
you saw.

In that moment, I knew my ambition had been met
To be a mother to someone so beautiful and brave
To guide you through life's many twists and turns
And to cherish every moment with you.

So I raise my eyes to the sky
And thank God for this precious gift
For the opportunity to love and care for you
And to be your mother forevermore.

Souls Laced

Your hand in mine, our fingers laced
You press my hand deep in the sheet
My right hand is yours
My left is buried in your hair
Your breath is warm on my neck
Almost a whisper
Your lips, your taste - it lingers
Your voice, your breath - is in the air
The passion in your eyes, as our souls meet
Each thrust is not enough
I crave you.
I taste you.
I want you so much.
We become one
You purr like a kitten as you collapse on my chest
Our hearts beating as melodious one
You don't have to say it
Language, words - they don't matter
Or souls have connected
This is the memory that replays
Every night
Every second
In my depths
- Our souls connected

Tattoos

Our matching tattoos symbolize
That memories are tattooed in our hearts
A permanent, unchanging prize
That time cannot tear apart

Inked upon our skin with care
A design that's etched in flesh and bone
Each line, each curve, a memory we share
An unspoken bond we call our own

As seasons come and seasons go
And days turn into months and years
Our tattoos remain, a constant flow
Of memories, laughter, and tears

The beauty of these tattoos lies
Not in the intricate design we chose
But in the messages they signify
Of love, of friendship, of life's woes

And though the years may take their toll
And our bodies may grow weak and old
Our matching tattoos, a shining soul
Will keep our memories from growing cold

So let us cherish what we've wrought
And treasure every memory we make
Our matching tattoos, a powerful thought
That from our hearts will never break.

Dark Horizon

The sun always rose over the horizon
Its warmth and light a sacred guise
But now the darkness is my companion
As memories of you slowly dies

You gave up on me, without a care
Our love a mere flicker in your heart
Now I'm left with pain hard to bear
As each day we drift further apart

The cycle of life still moves on
Even as joy and love take flight
The passage of time, never gone
Forever etched in day and night

The pain I feel, a constant refrain
An endless loop of despair and sorrow
For you, my love, will always remain
An unfulfilled promise for tomorrow

So as the sun sets on another day
And shadows cloak the earth in gloom
I'll pray for our love to find its way
And break free from this cycle of doom.

The Ballet

Our souls intertwined, a cosmic connection so true,
In an instant, we were drawn to each other like glue.
You were my sunshine, my moon, my stars up above,
I believed in us, our unbreakable love.

But on a villainous day, you betrayed me in the worst way,
My heart shattered, I was lost without a say.
I said goodbye, tried to move on from the pain,
Yet the universe had other plans, it brought you back again.

Each time we collide it's like déjà vu,
I'm reminded of the love we once knew.
Our souls still connected, I can't escape the pull,
It's like fate is trying to make us whole.

But my heart is hesitant, it's been burned before,
Can I trust you again or will you walk out the door?
I'm torn between the desire to love and protect,
Or to push you away and never look back.

Yet the cosmic power that binds us together,
Is too strong, too beautiful to sever.
We dance around each other, a cosmic ballet,
In this endless cycle, we seem doomed to stay.

Weeping Willow

The weeping willow whistles in the wind,
Its branches swaying to and fro.
Childhood memories come rushing in,
As I stand here below.

The smell of grandmother's perfume,
Brings back forgotten days.
The scent, like a sweet bloom,
Evokes her gentle ways.

Ancestors in the wind, whispers of old,
Their stories etched in the breeze.
Their spirits, forever bold,
Stirring up memories with ease.

The willow's song, a soothing sound,
Creating a sense of calm.
Its leaves rustle, dance around,
Like a healing balm.

Oh, how time has flown by,
Memories fading, like the setting sun.
But the willow's song, will always apply,
Echoes of love, forever spun.

The weeping willow whistles in the wind,
A constant reminder of treasures stored within.

Etches

It wasn't love we made, but still you stay
Etched in my soul, a mark no-one can erase
Our bodies intertwined, in passion's blaze
But in my heart, you've left a deeper trace

Your name carved deep, within my very being
Impressions lasting longer than mere skin
A memory I can't escape, though fleeting
With every thought, my spirit wears thin

The way we moved, beneath the moon's bright glow
The rhythm of our hearts, a lover's cadence
But in the end, it was just a show
Our flame extinguished, with no sense or senescence

Yet still you stay, with each and every breath
Your name a reminder of a moment's death

Threads of Time

Heartstrings wound tight within a spool,
Turning in time, never breaking the rule,
Each strand a memory, etched with care,
Stitched and sewn with such earthly flare.

Crystal glitter flickers in the hourglass,
A reminder that our time will come to pass,
Tick by tick, the grains of sand fall,
As our destiny slowly answers the call.

Shimmering glass reflects our inner being,
A soulful mirror for all our seeing,
Wrought from a fire, a passion within,
A flame that burns even in sin.

Death may take our physical form,
But these strings of love will help us transform,
Into the ether, a place of light,
Where our heartstrings hold us tight.

Our earthly threads may loosen and fray,
But our souls will forever stay,
Bound by love and pure devotion,
In an eternal, mystical ocean.

So let the spool keep turning in time,
As we write our story, page by rhyme,
With every strand, let love be our guide,
And in the end, we'll forever abide.

Peonies

In the garden, peonies grow
Their petals soft as morning dew
A feast to the eyes, a scent to know

A symphony of pink and white hue
Their beauty, fleeting, like a summer breeze
And yet, a memory they imbue

Of love that blooms, then gently leaves
Of moments shared, now lost in time
Of sweetness that, with time, recedes

Oh peonies, your fragrance sublime
A reminder of love's transient grace
Of moments that were once all mine

Now I watch as you wilt in their place
A symbol of time's unyielding flow
A fleeting reminder of loves that race

And yet, there's comfort, in this I know
That in seasons yet to come, you'll grow.

Phoenix and Lotus

No flame to light the skies
No resplendent phoenix to rise
Only darkness in sight, no hope
The heart is torn, too broken to cope

No chance to soar to new heights
No flicker of hope, no guiding lights
Only loneliness and despair in sight
The soul dark, clouded with blight

No dirt, no foundation to grow
No lotus to emerge and glow
Only emptiness in the heart
A life devoid of any part

Love, like fire, brings warmth and light
But, without it, darkness reigns in spite
Life, like dirt, provides a place to start
Without it, the heart is torn apart

A phoenix needs fire to rise anew
A lotus needs mud to grow and imbue
Love needs a chance to sparkle bright
A relationship needs a place to ignite

Thus, let us seek the fire to ignite
Let us find the mud for a new life
Let love bring warmth and light
Let relationships flourish, sans strife.

Pages of the Hourglass

Let our hearts beat with fire and passion,
As the sands of the hourglass fall,
For time is but a fleeting ration,
And precious moments pass us all.

Let us embrace every chapter,
In this tale that we call our life,
For each moment will become a treasure,
Through the joys and struggles of strife.

The pages turn with every breath,
As our story begins to take shape,
We are the heroes in this quest,
Fighting against fate's cruel games.

Our love, a shining light of hope,
That shall guide us through the darkest night,
No matter where the future slopes,
Our bond shall remain ever bright.

So let the hourglass turn its page,
And let us cherish every stage,
For though our time may slip away,
Our love and life will always stay.

Allah's Love

Amidst the chaos, two souls exist,
Destined to unify, heal and persist.
All diseases vanquished, at this union's behest,
But only if they combine, as offered by the Blessed.

No other way, exists for this miracle to occur,
Nine hundred and ninety-nine, souls must defer.
Their destiny, to perish, to pave the way,
For the ultimate vision, to come and stay.

Allah designed love, as a binding force,
Capable of breaking shackles, and charting a new course.
But the cost always great, a heavy price to pay,
The merging of souls, can never be child's play.

One soul left alone, for eternity to dwell,
The other departed, taking with it, the enchanting spell.
But what of the diseases, eradicated, and gone forever,
And the impact wrought, shall be known forever and ever.

A unique destiny, for those unifying souls,
A divine purpose, to cleanse and make whole.
In this union, immunity in its essence,
Bringing to fruition, Allah's benevolence.

So let us ponder, this unique phenomenon,
The power of love, and all that it has done.
May we emulate, this epic union of souls,
To live in harmony, and mend shattered goals.

Beautiful Embrace

In the air, whippoorwill's song rings clear
A haunting melody that fills my ear
Unfettered by the strains of life
It cuts through the noise, cuts like a knife

Simplicity is the beauty of a red-winged
blackbird
Flitting about, never preachy or absurd
In its humble way it speaks to me
Of life's joys, of life's simplicity

The snowberry clearwing flits with grace
A vision of beauty, a delight to embrace
Its wings flutter, as if to say
Life is fleeting, live it today

Oh, to be like these creatures so free
Unburdened by worries, unburdened by thee
To live, to love, to be without fear
This is what these creatures hold dear

Let us learn from them and take flight
Embrace life, embrace its might
Let simplicity lead us down the way
And find our joy in life's bouquet.

The Crescent Star of Türkiye

From the Black Sea to the turquoise dream,
Eyüp Sultan and apple tea,
Börek and döner, midye and dolma,
Hot tea grace the lips, may the Turkish coffee
tell my future.

Ferry on the Bosphorus, Galata Tower and Hagia
Sophia,
Mevlana and poetry all around,
The mountains kiss the sea and memories tattoo
me.

I am the ship, sailing through life's tides,
The waves of my mind crashing and rising high.

I am the apple, delicious and sweet,
Core to the soul, nourishing and complete.

I am the tea, hot and soothing,
Calm in a cup, a moment's peace of mind.

I am the coffee, strong and bold,
Awakening the senses, revealing truths untold.

I am the pastry, flaky and golden,
Melted cheese and savory filling,

Cracking open the layers of my heart,
Revealing the core, simple and pure.

I am the sea, vast and mysterious,
Waves crashing against the shore,

A reflection of the sky above,
Stretching towards infinity, eternity's core.

From the spiritual to the mundane,
Metaphor and imagery weave my story,
Echoing the words of Rumi,
Enshrining the mystery of existence's glory.

Country Heart

Whippoorwill's song in the hush of night,
Red-winged blackbird perched in flashing sight.
Owl on the fence post, calling to the moon,
Melodies of nature's timeless tune.

On the red dirt road, memories unfold,
Fluttering bald eagle, sun kissed and bold.

Fleeting moments etched in the mind,
Forever captured, forever entwined.

Cornbread in a cast iron, warm and sweet,
Sustenance for the soul, a delicious treat.

Dancing maple leaves on the path ahead,
A journey of life, both joyous and dread.

Moonlit crickets chirping in a faraway land,
Nature's symphony, a divine command.

Paradoxes hidden in every verse,
Love, religion, humanity, forever to traverse.

Equal number of words per line,
A format free, yet intricate and divine.
Metaphysical concepts abound,
Expanding the mind, lost and found.

Whippoorwill's song, red-winged blackbird in flight,
A world of wonder, an endless night.
Life's tapestry woven, colors so bright,
The human experience, a paradoxical sight.

The World Within The Wind

The wind holds a world within its grasp,
Ancestors' voices echo in its gasp,
Future children's earth, a dream to clasp,
Whippoorwill's last song, a haunting rasp.

The mockingbird's silence, a paradox rare,
Fragrant lilac fills the evening air,
The red sun kisses the mountain fair,
The moon lights the sea with gentle care.

A world between us, yet souls connect,
Eucalyptus refreshes, a breeze perfect,
Crickets in the cemetery, an eerie effect,
Embrace, our love, our hearts to protect.

The wind carries us, a mystery unexplained,
Love and religion intertwined, a bond retained,
Human experience, a journey sustained,
In the wind, a world forever maintained.

Nature's wonder, a beauty untamed,
And the wind carries on, with no end to its game.
It knows every secret and whispers in our hearts,
Guiding us through life, as it plays its part.

Printed in the USA
CPSIA information can be obtained
at www.ICGtesting.com
LVHW021822071223
765728LV00078B/2138

Printed in the USA
CPSIA information can be obtained
at www.ICGtesting.com
LVHW021822071223
765728LV00078B/2138